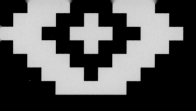

W9-BHI-142

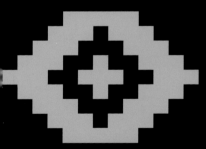

Introduction

The continent that pulsates to the fiery music of samba, tango, cumbia, and candombe provides an exciting environment for business as well. South America today bursts with opportunities for import, export, manufacturing, services, and supply. The tumultuous politics of the past are steadily giving way to government policies aligned to the needs of international business. Large numbers of hardworking people are enjoying their entry into the middle class. Their productivity is transforming abundant natural resources into increased GDP and pushing demand for the consumer goods they crave.

Doing Business in South America gives you the information and perspectives you need to survive and succeed in this exciting market. It tells you about the business context including history, opportunities, laws, and customs. It takes the vast diversity of culture and focuses on the most important features a newcomer should understand in order to build strong relationships. And it offers plenty of practical pointers for getting established on the ground.

Business opportunities of all kinds—from agriculture to software development—are springing up all across this large and varied continent. The land and its people offer rich rewards to organizations prepared to undertake expansion to the region, and to learn its ways of doing business. A truly diverse global portfolio needs to include South America. And managers heading to South America need this book.

Chapter 1

Business profile

South America offers the turbo-charged growth of newly industrialized economies with the comfortable familiarity of European roots. You can understand this unique combination through the region's history, political trends, and business characteristics, which explain how 13 distinct nations share the continent's geography, wealth, and potential.

Managing extremes

South America is characterized by extremes—lavish wealth and miserable poverty, dense urbanization and unexplored jungles, vast natural resources and innovative technological breakthroughs. To succeed in this region, managers must enter with an open mind and embrace the rich diversity.

PREPARE FOR VARIETY
Expect to use a range of business strategies in the region, to cope with the extreme contrasts in conditions.

Different countries

South America comprises 12 countries and one "overseas department" that can be roughly divided into three groups by language. Portuguese-speaking Brazil makes up about half the continent in size and population. Nine countries make up the Spanish-speaking group of South America, matching Brazil with a population of about 200 million. In the third group, at the far north, languages vary: the half a million people of Suriname speak Dutch, the 800,000 people of Guyana speak English, and the 250,000 people of French Guiana are actually French citizens.

Diverse populations

Besides indigenous peoples, South America is home to people from Africa, Asia, Europe, and the Middle East. More Japanese descendants live in Brazil than in any other place except Japan. The population density varies greatly. Each country of South America has sparsely populated expanses and one or two large population centers. Ecuador has the greatest population density with 138 people per square mile. Suriname, Guyana, and French Guiana have fewer than nine people per square mile.

Extremes of development

The per capita GDP of South American nations ranges from $4,000 in Paraguay to $14,300 in Chile, but the contrasts between the wealthy and poor are among the greatest on Earth. Every country falls between 40 and 60 by the Gini coefficient*, compared to the 20s and 30s in Europe. In human development, the countries are ranked between 40 (Chile) and 111 (Bolivia) among some 200 nations. In rural areas utilities such as electricity or paved roads may not be available. Yet the region produces automobiles and launches satellites.

*Gini coefficient—
The Gini coefficient is a ratio that represents the distribution of wealth in a country, where higher numbers reflect a greater difference between rich and poor.

IN FOCUS... GEOGRAPHICAL EXTREMES

The region's geography and climate are another source of its diversity. The Amazon is the Earth's largest rainforest and Atacama in southern Chile is the Earth's driest desert. The Andes is the Earth's longest mountain range. La Paz, Bolivia is the world's highest capital city. Cape Horn, Chile is only 805 km (500 miles) from Antarctica, and average temperatures are at freezing point throughout the winter. In contrast, half the countries of the continent are on or above the equator. Natural resources are equally varied, supporting a wide range of business types. Some of the land is rich in mineral resources, while others support large-scale agriculture.

Country profiles

South America is an important region for business, but it is not yet so integrated that you can apply a uniform strategy. Consider your options country by country. The five largest economies that are open to global business are highlighted here. But don't neglect to investigate some of the smaller countries that might match a particular focus of your strategy.

Brazil

Capital/largest city: **Brasília/São Paulo**

Population: **200 million**

Official language: **Portuguese**

GDP/GDP per capita: **$1.7 billion (2008)/$10,100 (purchasing power parity)**

Currency: **1 real (BRL) = 100 centavos**

Time zone: **UTC -2 to -4**

Dialing code: **+55**

Principal business areas: **São Paulo, Rio de Janeiro, Campinas, Porto Alegre**

Brazil is the largest country in the region in terms of area, population, and economy. It is ranked as the world's 10th largest economy by the International Monetary Fund and the World Bank. Its economy spans agriculture, mining, industry, and technological services as well as a large pool of labor. Brazilian exports are booming, creating a new generation of tycoons. Major export products include aircraft, coffee, automobiles, steel, ethanol, and electrical equipment. Brazil is regarded as one of the four fastest emerging economies alongside Russia, India, and China.

Chile

Capital/largest city: **Santiago/Santiago**

Population: **17 million**

GDP/GDP per capita: **$181 billion (2008)/$14,700 (purchasing power parity)**

Currency: **1 peso (CLP) = 100 centavos**

Time zone: **UTC -4**

Principal business areas: **Santiago, Valparaíso**

Chile is one of South America's most stable nations. Business-friendly government policies drive the economy. Chile's economy is split almost evenly between industry and services, with agriculture a distant third. Important sectors include aircraft manufacture, copper, mining, and financial services.

Argentina

Capital/largest city: **Buenos Aires/Buenos Aires**

Population: **40 million**

GDP/GDP per capita: **$339 billion (2008)/$14,400 (purchasing power parity)**

Currency: **1 peso (ARS) = 100 centavos**

Time zone: **UTC -3**

Principal business areas: **Buenos Aires, Córdoba, Rosario, Mendoza**

Manufacturing is the nation's largest sector, especially in the areas of food processing, chemicals, and machine and automotive parts. Argentina is also one of the world's major agricultural producers, with soy farming, beef and dairy herds, and sheep farming as significant contributors to the economy.

Peru

Capital/largest city: **Lima/Lima**

Population: **30 million**

GDP/GDP per capita: **$107 billion (2008)/$7,800 (purchasing power parity)**

Currency: **1 nuevo sol (PEN) = 100 céntimos**

Time zone: **UTC -5**

Principal business areas: **Lima, Cajamarca, Ica, Cuzco**

Peru's economy is largely based on services, which account for over half of its GDP. Other important contributors are mining and the processing of metals and fossil fuels, and automotive manufacture. Peru's main exports are copper, gold, zinc, textiles, and fish meal.

Colombia

Capital/largest city: **Bogotá/Bogotá**

Population: **46 million**

GDP/GDP per capita: **$202 billion (2008)/$8,000 (purchasing power parity)**

Currency: **1 peso (COP) = 100 centavos**

Time zone: **UTC -5**

Principal business areas: **Bogotá, Medellín, Santiago de Cali**

The Colombian economy has one of the highest growth rates in South America, reaching 8.2 percent in 2007. Its main industries are agriculture—largely coffee—and mining—mostly coal, petroleum products, and gold. Tourism is also increasingly important to the Colombian economy.

Choosing South America

South America should be a part of any internationally diversified business portfolio. Its growing population, burgeoning economy, top educational institutions, and largely untapped human capital provide all the fundamentals for solid business. The maturing governments of the region have built stable economies that welcome international partners.

Developing economies

*GDP — *Gross Domestic Product is a measure of a country's economic performance based on the value of goods and services it produces.*

South American countries have achieved fast growth and stability. In the last few years, Argentina, Colombia, Peru, Uruguay, and Venezuela have all achieved an annual GDP* growth of seven percent or more for multiple years. Business-friendly policies are promoting rapid economic expansion in Chile, Uruguay, Brazil, Colombia, and Peru. These countries are leading the region in improved transparency, reduced bureaucracy, and solid fiscal policies. New trade agreements are being negotiated and signed at an accelerated pace. Compared to other growth regions of the world, South America has a solid foundation for international business that minimizes risks and ensures sustainability.

IN FOCUS... A GROWING MARKET

In comparison to the US and EU, South America's population is significantly younger and still growing, with more than 25 percent of its people under 15 years of age. The increasing size of the market makes South America attractive, but it is the increasing wealth that makes the market so promising. In recent years, consumers have been getting richer, with countries in the region being re-classified from low-income to middle-income economies. The regional GDP is about \$2.3 billion, adjusted for purchasing power parity (PPP) to \$3.7 billion. This boom happened so quickly that supply for consumer goods has not kept up with demand.

Winning with South America

FAST GROWING ECONOMIES
- Several South American countries have achieved GDP growth of 7 per cent
- Business-friendly policies are promoting rapid economic expansion
- They show improved transparency, reduced bureaucracy, and solid fiscal policies

WIDE RANGE OF INDUSTRIES
- Diverse economies are not dependent on commodity-based exports
- Imports and exports total $450 billion and $550 billion respectively
- South America was remarkably resilient during the economic crisis of 2008

PROXIMITY OF CULTURE AND GEOGRAPHY
- Ethnically varied population makes it easy for international partners to find a cultural match
- Cultural proximity helps you to understand local business culture and communication styles
- Shipping routes from South America to Europe and North America are shorter than those from East Asia

History and business

The history of South America has often been tumultuous and violent, but the drive to progress and peace always reasserts itself. With 13 countries on the continent and dozens of indigenous groups, this brief history of the region will focus on broad trends and their general economic impacts.

Colonizing the region

*Encomienda system—*the Spanish policy of giving power over a tract of land to a loyal subject, who could use the people on it for labor and teach them Spanish and Roman Catholicism.*

Before Europeans set foot on the continent, many diverse peoples such as the Inca, Muisca, and Chavin lived here. There is evidence of established trade, agriculture, and finely-crafted arts. Spain and Portugal established South American settlements in the 1500s. European colonization changed the dynamics of the region. Indigenous peoples were conquered and used for labor under the "encomienda" system*. A huge gap in wealth between the rich and the poor was established at this time.

CULTURAL ANTENNAE

Leaning left

Talk of a unified western hemisphere with US leadership fizzled out in the first years of the 21st century. One by one, free-trade capitalist politicians were voted out and replaced by a new brand of socialist–populist presidents in the model of Venezuela's Hugo Chavez. Some of these governments have assumed control of private industries from oil to rice processing. Several firms have lost their assets in these sweeping acts of national reform. Despite the move to the left, South America for the most part still embraces free market policies and is working toward greater continental integration.

Populism and dictatorships

A series of revolutions and treaties in the 19th century brought an end to colonization in the region. As the World Wars and Cold War redefined global politics and economics, South American nations ricocheted between political extremes. The wealthy few still dominated, and civil unrest led to frequent changes of government in the late 1800s and early 1900s. By the mid-1900s, much of the region was ruled by dictatorships. The economic path of South America at this time was toward protectionist trade policies and strict import controls to promote rapid industrial development. Governments scrambled for control, managing state-owned industries to create jobs and local wealth. This economic transformation was largely funded by loans from foreign countries seeking geopolitical influence. Hyper-inflation soared, with annual rates of 3,000 percent and more in some countries. Guerilla groups violently fought repression and capitalist inequality.

Making way for democracy

The transitions from dictatorships to democracies in the 1980s were sometimes violent victories and sometimes more like exhausted surrenders. Investigations into the disappearances, tortures, and other abuses of the 1980s are largely unresolved and lingering resentments and distrust of government still simmer. Restored democracies in the 1990s promoted capitalism as the path to economic stability and wealth creation. Economic liberalization provided growth opportunities for foreign firms and jobs for locals. Competitive imports brought an array of merchandise and new technologies to consumers. Inflation dropped to single digits, economies stabilized, and industries diversified.

Adjusting to rapid change

Managing in South America is a balancing act that requires agility, flexibility, optimism, realism, and sometimes a good sense of humor. Change can be rapid and radical in this part of the world, and businesses must react quickly to avoid disaster and embrace opportunity.

TRY NEW STRATEGIES

Be prepared to try new strategies to reach South American consumers. It may be hard to let go of conventional wisdom, but novel strategies can work very well in this diverse market.

Expecting the unexpected

Dramatic changes are the norm in South America. Politics in the region have been consistently tumultuous: Argentina once had five presidents in two weeks. Extreme weather shifts and inadequate infrastructure also cause dramatic interruptions. A popular joke claims this is the land of tomorrow, but tomorrow is always in the future. In this volatile climate, the most valued skills are related to building relationships and adapting to change. Due to constant uncertainty, plans are less important than crisis management.

ENSURING SUCCESS

FAST TRACK	OFF TRACK
Building a network of relationships	Ignoring social groups
Planning optimistically and adapting strategically	Making rigid plans and sticking to them
Responding swiftly and innovatively to rapid changes	Failing to pick up cues from the immediate environment
Focusing on having the right people instead of the right plan	Not trusting local people: keeping them out of top positions

Managing crises

TIP

RESPOND TO CHANGE
Leverage changes as they happen, and make your adaptations strategically not randomly.

Successful managers in South America expect uncertainty to be a daily occurrence, not an occasional event. They face disruptive trade disputes, lengthy labor strikes, floods and landslides, volatile politics, privatizations and expropriations. Organizations have to react quickly to survive. To draw an analogy with a game of soccer, strategy is not mapped on a grid, but is developed by training the team in practice so that they can act during the game to quickly analyze a situation, react swiftly, and work together cooperatively.

Cooperating to succeed

South American managers must know whom they can trust. In uncertainty, in upheaval, and in hope, it is relationships that provide security, partners who cooperate in crisis, and friends who share the victories. In 1990 when Fernando Collor, the President of Brazil, froze personal and corporate bank accounts across Brazil, managers turned to a network of relationships and survived the 18-month freeze through a system of barter. A business network is not a collection of business cards, but a lifetime of friendships and bonds of mutual confidence.

CASE STUDY

Corporate agility
South America is Avon's biggest market. The company's personal selling model allows them to respond quickly to economic changes. When times are good, people buy more cosmetics. When times are bad, more people sell to supplement their incomes, and the company makes it easy to get started. The model provides agility for payments. One sales representative in the Amazon will accept a chicken in trade for a lipstick and then pay the company in cash. Sales representatives are also trained to educate women about current health issues, providing a vital service.

Finding opportunities

The traditional mineral and agricultural riches of the continent continue to be important, but rapid socioeconomic advances, technological innovations, and infrastructure priorities are creating new opportunities for business success in the region.

Finding import and export opportunities

Exports to South America are driven by the fast-growing middle-class market and growing demand for consumer products. Manufacturers in the region are also racing to catch up, so opportunities for selling to them are abundant. Imports from the region are most attractive when exchange rates are favorable. Abundant natural resources and production advantages make South American products a good choice for export. Technological advances in manufacturing ensure that the quality of local products meets export standards.

LOW INCOME
Companies willing to adjust their products and prices can tap into a huge market among the region's poorer classes.

TECHNOLOGY
Software development and new technology are the region's focus for future prominence and efficiency.

NATURAL PRODUCTS
South America supplies natural and "fair-trade" products for wealthy nations that shop according to their values.

Forming partnerships

Many major South American companies are going global on their own, and these pioneers have opened the way for smaller companies to follow. However, smaller companies often do not have the resources to enter the global arena by themselves. Many are eager to form partnerships with other companies in their target countries as a way of reducing risks and increasing opportunities for learning when expanding internationally.

Identifying key business opportunities in South America

INFRASTRUCTURE
Government contracts can be big. Public–private partnerships such as toll highways are on the rise.

INDUSTRIAL GOODS
Manufacturing companies are seeking state-of-the-art equipment to support their expansion.

MID-SIZE MARKETS
The big cities are quite saturated. But second-tier cities are eager for consumer products and services.

CONSUMER PRODUCTS
A rapidly expanding middle class is eagerly pursuing the good life they have seen on TV.

Going global

At one time, South America's natural resources provided its primary economic link to other global regions. But now its manufacturing base is strengthening, its consumer market is growing, and its industries are diversifying. South America's role on the world stage has moved far beyond the commodities exports of earlier years.

TIP

USE EXISTING LINKS
Take advantage of established diplomatic and business links to find your way into South America.

North America

South America's largest trading partner is the United States. Proposed economic integration through a Free Trade Alliance of the Americas has been given up due to waning US influence in the region. However, the US is still a large consumer of South American agricultural and mineral products, and a major source of foreign direct investment. Of late, US companies are not just buying the region's agricultural produce but are buying the land also so that they own production capacity.

CASE STUDY

Brazilian company goes global
Natura launched its eco-friendly cosmetics lines in Brazil in 1969 and managed its international expansion from the familiar to the distant. The company expanded into Chile in 1982. After an unsuccessful stint in the US, the company moved into another South American neighbor, Bolivia. Natura spread still further, to Argentina, Mexico, Colombia, and Venezuela. In 2002, the company began retailing at Brazilian airports. Success in selling to tourists led to a shop in Paris, and then expansion to other parts of Europe and to Japan.

Europe

Colonization by Spain and Portugal saw immigrants from Europe settling in South America. As their descendents have built successful businesses in the region, many look to their family homelands for global partners. Exports, subsidiaries, and joint ventures are found across the Atlantic, with movement both ways. Trade with Europe provides a large market for export, high-quality goods for import, and business partners who are well funded and efficient.

The rest of the world

Russia and China serve as a counterpoint to the influence of the US in the region. When political differences made trade with the US untenable, countries like Venezuala turned to Russia. Russian influence is strong when its economy is strong, but China is a new alternative. China is pouring money into South American economies to create infrastructure and to secure supplies of resources like oil, iron ore, and soya for its fast-growing demands. The Middle East has ties to South America through immigration that led to both import and export. Slavery brought many Africans to South America, but the two regions do not share much economically— both regions look to wealthier partners for their business focus.

Latin America

Latin America is made up of the western hemisphere countries colonized by Spain and Portugal. These countries are bound by historical and cultural similarities, and includes Mexico, Central America, many Caribbean nations, and the South American nations. Countries in this region are increasing trade with one another. Companies are exporting and partnering throughout the region in a wide range of industries including aircraft design, cosmetics, beverage, and retail.

Understanding the workforce

The large difference between the resources available to the wealthy and the poor produces an unevenly prepared workforce. The highest tiers of a company will have skills and training equal to those in top business centers anywhere, but low-skilled workers may be less prepared for their responsibilities than those in other regions.

Appreciating executives

Most South American executives are well trained and well traveled; do not underestimate them. Assess executives not by their company sales figures but by getting to know their professional challenges and successes. Having succeeded in difficult conditions, South American executives are shrewd strategists and sharply observant. The local laws may also encourage them to be more aggressive competitors than those in your home country. Develop friendly professional relationships based on mutual respect.

Laborers and office workers

Experienced South American industrial workers are productive, clever, and innovative. They may prefer convenience or speed to established procedures. This can improve efficiency, but make sure safety and quality are not compromised. Labor movements and strikes are not uncommon in South America and can be disruptive to business. Despite an adversarial stance between labor and management, cooperation and trust can keep things calm. Hiring procedures should verify required skills. A high school diploma is not a guarantee of basic math and language skills. Company-sponsored training can be a smart investment in human capital.

Budgeting for labor

Many laws and regulations favor workers, making layoffs costly. You could hire inexperienced labor, but considerable resources will have to be spent on training. Labor in South America may be cheap, but a low hourly wage does not represent the true picture. Each country adds its own extras such as retirement funds, supplements for necessities, and taxes that support social programs. As an employer, you may be expected to contribute to any or all of these.

TIP

FACTOR IN BENEFITS
Wages and benefits are calculated per month. Benefits may cost about the same as an employee's salary, doubling the labor cost.

BUDGETING FOR LABOR BENEFITS IN BRAZIL

INDIVIDUAL BENEFIT	AMOUNT	ANNUAL COST ESTIMATE IN REAIS
Minimum wage	about $465/month	5,580
Meal supplement	about $5/day	1,260
Transportation supplement	about $4/day	1,008
Individual emergency account	8%	446
Individual retirement account	20%	1,116
Insurance	2%	112
Child education supplement (up to 7 years of age)	2.5%	140
"13th salary" vacation supplement	one month	465
Vacation supplement	one-third of one month	153
Agrarian reform fund tax (INCRA)	0.2%	11
Worker social fund tax (SESI/SESC)	1.5%	84
Worker training fund tax (SENAI)	1.0%	56
Small business fund tax (SEBRAE)	0.6%	33

Identifying types of business

You will encounter a wide variety of business types in South America. Almost any retail district in the region will host both big global brands and small local players. There are some business types here that you will find elsewhere, and also some that are uniquely South American.

DO YOUR HOMEWORK
Before entering the South American market, conduct thorough research of all the possible competition you will face and work out strategies to deal with them.

Dealing with local competition

Foreign-owned companies are generally welcome in the region as they are expected to bring cash, technology, and jobs. You can leverage these expectations to compete with local firms, by offering good salaries and working conditions, or encouraging customers with active marketing. However, don't expect your foreign passport to open all doors. Even small local companies can be fierce competitors where they are part of local networks and have strong relationships with retailers, consumers, and the government. Don't underestimate customer and employee loyalty.

Handling global competition

Some major businesses that operate in other parts of the world are also strong players in South America. These are multinationals whose approach you can predict fairly well from their actions in other regions. In South America, some multinationals have penetrated the market so completely that their sectors are virtually closed to new entrants—traditional banking is one example. Of course, all for-profit companies have similar business reasons for partnering, competing, investing, and entrenching. However, not all companies approach their business decisions with the same motives and focus. Choose your entry point carefully and research the strong players, whether they be local or global.

Knowing the competition

- **Multi-Latinas** Dominant in their home countries, expansion within the continent is a next step for growth. Partnering with these companies may speed your own expansion in the region.
- **"Grupos"** Large, privately-owned conglomerates may have subsidiaries across dozens of different industries that provide supplies and services for one another. Don't even try to provide a grupo member with anything the grupo can provide for itself. However, successfully working with one branch can open opportunities with all the others.
- **Family businesses** These can be small and medium companies or large conglomerates. Establishing good relations with the family may be more important than promising financial returns. Giving back to the community is a strong priority for such firms, with benefits to the family reputation and social capital.
- **Local stalwarts** If looking to expand in mid-size cities of South America, watch out for regional players. They can be surprisingly powerful due to their tight relationships with retail partners and consumers.
- **Latina multinationals** These companies are building partnerships and opening subsidiaries in Europe, Asia, and the Middle East. Your first point of contact may be in your own market or in a third country.

TIP

KNOW THE GEOGRAPHY
Research the reach of your competitors. Multi-Latinas operate across several South American countries, so be aware that their power base can be far from where you meet them.

IN FOCUS... INFORMAL COMPETITORS

While doing business in South America, be prepared for competition from unexpected quarters. One competitive challenge is bidding against companies or individuals that can undercut your offer because they may not be paying taxes or complying with government regulations. You may also find your competition coming from unexpected quarters—like suppliers of herbal remedies instead of pharmaceuticals, and neighborhood bakeries that sell convenience items like milk, toothpaste, and diapers, in competition with supermarkets.

Accepting responsibility

Organizations operate under implicit social pacts. They have the right to make a profit in exchange for providing services to society. In some countries, companies are only expected to contribute economically. In South America, social expectations of organizations include social welfare.

Understanding needs

Although all South American countries have social welfare programs, basic needs are not met for many people. Estimates are that 60 percent of Bolivians, 50 percent of Peruvians, and 40 percent of Venezuelans live in poverty. The middle classes in Brazil and Chile have grown, but even in these emerging economies, many lead hard lives. Few people starve, but many are undernourished, uneducated, and unemployed.

Creative corporate social responsibility

HEALTH
Door-to-door sales representatives give health tips during sales visits

Giving back to society

Besides paying taxes, making products, and causing people no harm, organizations in the region are expected to improve people's lives. They should provide for their workers through food, transportation, and healthcare, and give back to the communities in which they operate through roads, meal programs, and education. Where governments cannot do enough, organizations are expected to provide assistance.

TIP

PARTNER WITH LOCAL CHARITIES
Small, local charities can be good partners in social projects. Involve your employees as well as giving donations to ensure visibility, sustainability, and employee morale.

Reaping the benefits

PR benefits are among the most obvious reasons for community involvement in South America. Many companies display the logos of the charities and social projects they assist. These feature in company films, fliers, and news stories. They improve public perception of an organization. Employee morale and respect are additional benefits. Giving employees a chance to serve their community shifts their affiliation with the organization from purely financial to emotional as well.

NUTRITION
Company cafeteria offers free meal program to local schools

RESOURCES
End-of-spool yarn donated to local families to make baby sweaters

SKILLS
Company restaurant staff teach local restaurateurs catering skills

Chapter 2

Understanding business etiquette

This chapter outlines the essentials for establishing good relationships—so important for success in South America. Learn to understand and respect local values, approaches, communication styles, and workplace expectations.

Managing particularism

Particularism is characteristic of South American ways of doing business. A particularist culture looks at every event as a unique case that must be considered individually. The contrasting approach is universalism, which assumes that all cases fall under general rules that apply all the time.

TIP

BE AN ALL-WEATHER FRIEND

Maintaining a positive personal relationship with suppliers is a good way to stay high on their list of priorities.

Understanding particularism

In universalist cultures, like the US, the UK, and much of northern Europe, signed contracts are firm commitments. But in particularist cultures, like South America, the specific circumstance must be considered to determine whether a clause still applies. Missing a contracted delivery time could be a point of conflict. The universalist culture expects delivery under any circumstances. This is unreasonable to the particularist. The particularist culture expects delivery as long as there are no unforeseen difficulties. This is irresponsible to the universalist.

Building trust

To manage particularism, partners must trust one another and work together to create alternative solutions. You should ensure that your partners are involved in the success of your organization, and know that the terms of your contract are not arbitrary, but are an essential part of the operation. Involving partners in the whole process, and making them feel a shared responsibility for the total outcome, will encourage them to produce timely solutions to obstacles.

TIP

HAVE A BACK-UP
There may be times when dramatic events make progress impossible. An alternate supplier, back-up stock, or a flexible schedule can be invaluable in such emergencies.

Getting the best service

In particularist cultures, you should ensure that you are at the top of your partner's list of priorities. One way to do this is to stay on their radar. Don't wait until 5pm on Monday to check on a delivery that was expected at noon. Call on Friday and ask if everything is on schedule. Call again on Monday morning to remind the partner how important the delivery is. When problems arise, offer help rather than criticism. If you react harshly, partners may only inform you about future problems after they have become critical.

CULTURAL ANTENNAE

Particularism vs universalism

In the mid-afternoon heat of Salvador, Bahia, Brazil, a woman sat down at an empty patio table and was met by the waiter who took her drink order. Hungry, she asked for a menu, which the waiter quickly delivered. The woman made her selection and called the waiter back to take her order. The waiter replied, "I'm sorry, the kitchen is closed." "But if the kitchen is closed, why did you bring me the menu?" The waiter explained simply, "Because you asked." The woman assumed everyone asking for a menu wants to order food—a universal case. The waiter assumed each person asking for a menu has their own reasons and so complied with the woman's request—a particular case. The waiter could not be expected to know she was hungry.

Communicating effectively

Many people outside of the region do not realize that Spanish is not the only official language in South America. Brazil uses Portuguese, French Guiana uses French, and Suriname's official language is Dutch. And besides the languages, newcomers to the region need to understand the style of conversations and the use of non-verbal communication.

TIP

MAKE TIME FOR CHAT
Spend the first part of a meeting chatting with one another to catch up on family news, or discuss the latest soccer match. This informal conversation produces goodwill and makes friends.

Conversing in local language

Learning at least a few polite greetings and courtesies in local languages goes a long way with South Americans, even if you rely on a translator for the greater part of communication. Most South American executives who are university educated will speak a foreign language in addition to their native language. This is often English, though it may also be French, Italian, or German. However, even executives who can make themselves understood clearly in another language may feel self-conscious if they think they are not perfectly fluent or have a strong accent.

cuidado!

obrigado

tudo bom?

até logo!

Going with the flow

Conversations and even formal negotiations in South America tend to wander through many detours. The shape of a discussion is not as deliberate as the circular conversation patterns of Asia or the point-by-point conversations of Anglo cultures. It may be necessary to write down reminders about points that are left undecided so that you can return to them later. It is far better to go with the flow and build on shared energy than to insist on a planned agenda. The flow of conversation is one way a South American will determine whether someone is a good person to do business with. If conversation flows easily, this bodes well for a constructive friendship or business association.

IN FOCUS...
BRAZILIAN PORTUGUESE

Brazil is the single largest nation in the region, with over 180 million Portuguese speakers. Brazilians know their language is unusual in the region, but they also know they are the most populous country in South America, and prefer packaging instructions and labels to be printed in their own language. If space constraints or costs make that impossible, at least the main points of labels should be printed in both Spanish and Portuguese. Spanish speakers will find their language skills useful in Brazil, but it will be appreciated if you make the effort to learn at least a few basic Portuguese phrases, and apologize for speaking Spanish to Brazilian contacts.

hola!

¿cómo te llamas?

boa sorte!

salud!

encantado!

AVOID VERBAL COMPLAINT

South Americans tend to avoid direct conflict in conversation. A carefully worded, polite written complaint may work better than a face-to-face confrontation.

Expressing emotions

South Americans are emotionally expressive when they talk. More reserved cultures may mistake raised voices and hand-waving for anger or negative emotions, but such gestures are rarely threatening or directed at someone in particular. Gentle pokes to the chest or tugs on the arm will be made for emphasis and to keep attention, not to threaten or intimidate. Anger is rarely expressed in business conversations. The general volume of conversation in South America may seem like yelling, but tone rather than volume should be used to identify the emotion of a speaker. In a culture that prioritizes relationships, it is important to spend some time talking as friends before getting down to serious business. Starting a meeting by announcing the objectives is considered cold and formal.

JUMP INTO CONVERSATIONS

Speakers overlap one another's sentences in conversation, so don't wait for a pause to join a discussion.

Greeting appropriately

In every culture there is a distance between people that is considered professional, another that is considered friendly, and the closest that is considered intimate. South American friendly distance is more like the intimate distance of US and European cultures. A kiss on each cheek is the standard greeting between women who are friends and between women and men. Men shake hands and may grasp their partner's elbow or shoulder to express greater friendship. The South American kiss is more a gentle touching of cheeks than lips to cheeks. Remember that South Americans like to be friends with their co-workers and partners, so if a South American leans forward to kiss a cheek, that's a positive sign of a good working relationship. Flinching instead of welcoming this gesture may seem cold or unfriendly. Making the rounds of a table to greet each person individually makes each person feel important.

BUILDING RELATIONSHIPS

FAST TRACK	OFF TRACK
Greeting all members of a group individually	Flinching away from a greeting kiss instead of welcoming it
Opening a meeting with informal conversation	Assuming loud voices indicate anger or annoyance
Taking a relaxed attitude to physical contact and raised voices	Feeling annoyed or threatened by shrinking personal space
Looking out for subtext if answers seem evasive or unclear	Attempting to keep personal and business relationships separate

Understanding "no"

Communication in South America is high energy and high drama. To understand someone, you must pay attention to their tone of voice and body language. In South America, disagreement is often expressed with polite words of agreement stated with a flat reserve and negative facial expressions or body gestures. "Yes, some day we should talk about going into business together when we are not so busy with our other concerns" really means, "We have other concerns right now and should not talk about doing business together." When in doubt, a follow-up call will make the intention clear. Avoiding calls, changing the subject, and talking in broad general terms without ever getting to specifics are all polite ways to say no. Don't think of a polite "no" as "giving you the runaround." The true intention is to say no while still maintaining the friendship and keeping communication open.

Appreciating family ties

The extended family is the core structural unit of South American society and is central to all activities. Though friendship is also essential for business success, for most people in the region, friends are actually the second most important business asset. Family always comes first.

Getting to know the family

Talk about family is welcome in South America. The informal conversation at the beginning of a meeting often includes questions about one's family. This is not intrusive or getting "too personal." Small talk about a child's soccer match is not too small. Discussing friends and family is a way of discovering important mutual connections, and shared connections build trust. They imply an extended commitment to one another, and shared values and priorities. Talk of mutual interests outside work may lead to invitations to socialize together, and refusing these invitations may slow the progress toward strong business relationships.

Using family names

The most important information in a person's résumé is not their job title or corporate affiliation, it is the family name. It is one reason South Americans use multiple last names. The list of last names tells about a person's roots, the father's family, the mother's family, the family one has married into, even a family's origin before migrating to the Americas. The last name is like the list of schools one puts on a résumé.

CULTURAL ANTENNAE

Giving gifts

Gift giving is common in South American business, especially at first meetings. Gifts should be wrapped and include a personal touch like your company logo, something from your home country, or something you chose because it is your personal favorite. Candy, music, office items, or a scarf are good choices. Making a personal connection is more important than the price or brand. A gift for the secretary should not be as expensive as a gift for the boss. Do bring something for the spouse or kids if you meet the family.

Returning hospitality

As a business partner you should reciprocate social invitations, even if you are staying in a hotel. You could invite your hosts to a restaurant or to visit your family when in your home country. Reciprocating hospitality is not a matter of showing off your status; it is to make a gift of time and friendship to your business partners. Social time is valuable for business because it lets people get to know each other better, and build trust.

Knowing your place

South America is considered a high power-distance* culture. While formal power is respected in all cultures (corporate presidents have more power than janitors all over the world), in some cultures the formal power of the office spills into non-work situations as well. A person's title, office, and family network can attract a great deal of respect and deference.

Matching job titles

*Power-distance—
the extent to which
less powerful
members of an
organization display
social deference to
their superiors.

Low power-distance cultures tend to select their representatives for a task based on expertise. High power-distance cultures try to match the level of their representative to the representative they will be meeting. In a low power-distance culture, an IT technician can talk directly with a customer's vice president, but in a high power-distance culture, a vice president should meet with a vice president. It is not uncommon for people to come to meetings with a small entourage. This shows a person's status by exhibiting how many people she or he commands. It also ensures that the people with the necessary technical expertise are on hand when the official emissary needs assistance.

IN FOCUS... CHAIN OF COMMAND

Decisions in South America follow a chain of command. Managers communicate with other managers at their own level. It is appropriate to move up a chain of command in one's own unit and leave cross-unit discussions for higher level managers. Decisions come from the top. Senior managers will gather the information they need, solicit input, and consult trusted advisors. Their decisions filter back down through the organization. Sometimes a decision may be delayed because the person dealing with the matter does not have the authority to decide about it. It is useful to identify the key decision maker, so you can contact them directly or through your same-level representative. This is where positive social relationships pay off.

n high power-distance cultures like South America, everyone knows their proper place in relation to others. In initial meetings, people often arrange business cards they receive on the table in front of them and refer to them as the meeting progresses. This provides information about the names and status of whoever is speaking, and how they should be answered.

More important people should be allowed to speak first and should not be interrupted. They may not say much of substance in the beginning, but senior people set the tone of the meeting with polite welcomes, a review of the history of a partnership, and other background to the present meeting. A reciprocal introductory speech, filled with thanks, by a senior person on the other party is appropriate before getting down to business. Less senior people should defer to their seniors in discussions and keep their comments brief and polite. Warm greetings and big gestures may give the impression of informality, but business meetings are thoughtfully conducted.

REMEMBER TITLES

Take note of titles given on business cards during introductions. Try to build up a mental map of the power relationships between people you meet, and treat them accordingly.

Joining the team

Teamwork in South America is more than cooperation; it is a shared identity. Group members act together, reason together, produce together. South America is a collectivist culture, where primacy is given to group welfare. This contrasts with individualist cultures, where people work in a team by dividing tasks, acting separately, and blending the results later.

Sharing responsiblity

Groups share responsibilities, and the same task may be handled by several team members. The job descriptions are much more fluid in collectivist cultures. You may pick up more work today and be absolutely confident your teammate will do the extra next time. You are expected to show loyalty to your own group, bond socially, and shoulder the burdens of your colleagues. But this intense cooperation is focused on immediate working teams and does not extend to everyone in the same company.

ALWAYS WORK AS A UNIT
Each member of the team adds their own contribution. Try not to compare individual performances.

Navigating team roles

Sharing of duties may make it difficult for an outsider to figure out how to get help. One day you may be working with Maria, and the next day it could be Javier who returns your call, so be prepared to explain the situation again. The advantage of this team approach is that there is always someone available to answer your call. The team approach may make it seem that no one is responsible for getting the work done. If you find yourself stuck in this way, try tapping into the hierarchy at a higher point—it may get you the attention you need.

LEARN THE CULTURE
Follow local preferences, but don't stereotype. Get to know individuals and adjust to their preferred style.

WEAR THE TEAM SHIRT
Share responsibilites to integrate well in a group. Treat the burdens of your colleague as your own.

Surviving as a newcomer

SOCIALIZE AFTER WORK
Be part of a common social group to bring your work partners closer. Networking is a sure recipe for success.

ACCEPT YOUR ORIGIN
Don't be offended when you are labeled as a foreigner but make it clear that your origin is only one of your identities.

Motivating through respect

Respect is paramount to work motivation at all levels in South America. People want to be part of a company that treats them with personal attention and brings them admiration outside work. If your workers feel respected, they will work as if they were part owners of the company—they will identify with its success and protect it from failure.

TIP

CONSIDER COMPANY UNIFORMS

In conditions of high unemployment, wearing a company uniform can be a source of pride for your workforce, as it shows others that they have a stable job.

Respecting executives

To earn dedication from upper-level managers, make them feel like strategic partners. Show respect by keeping them informed of key decisions; they should not find them out from business journals.They want to be trusted as part of the inner circle, as close as possible to the people at the top. The best way to kill motivation in executives is to leave them stagnating in the same position while others are moving around them. Be clear about performance expectations but also about promotion opportunities. And, of course, provide dignified salaries, prestigious titles, and visible status symbols. Show respect for your executives in a way that makes them respected by others.

CASE STUDY

Monitoring staff motivation
Lear, a supplier of car seats for Volkswagen in São Jose de Campos, Brazil, has a magnetic chart posted prominently at the employee entrance. As they start the workday, everyone posts a magnetic face next to their photo—happy, neutral, or sad. People pay attention to the faces and give special attention to colleagues with a sad face. Managers are required to inquire about the concerns of employees who post a sad face. And managers receive the same caring treatment from their co-workers. Although most of the issues are personal and beyond the company's control, having a manager express personal interest shows great respect and makes the company a personal place to work. The workplace becomes a place to share one's joys and find sympathy for one's sorrows.

Rewarding line workers

Instead of competing for line workers by increasing salaries, consider other benefits that improve their quality of life and secure their loyalty. Providing on-site child care costs less per employee than a salary increase to cover individual child care. Subsidized housing near the plant can reduce travel time and stress for workers. Ensure that you have enough managers on the shop floor to know every worker by name and to keep up with their basic family news.

> **? ASK YOURSELF...**
> ## ARE YOU SHOWING RESPECT TO YOUR EMPLOYEES?
>
> - Do you involve your senior managers in the decision-making of the company?
> - Do you encourage upward communication and allow your employees to speak directly to their managers?
> - Are you taking steps to make your employees feel safe in their jobs?
> - Do you recognize people from all levels of the organizations individually and greet them personally?

Indirect communication

One consequence of the priority given to respect is that employees may be reluctant to criticize or disagree directly with their bosses. Everyone has seen a friend fired suddenly as a scapegoat. It is better to watch quietly as the boss makes a mistake than risk their anger by showing them the error. Instead, messages may pass up the chain indirectly —someone may tell you about something they have heard, rather than expressing their own opinion, or they will mention something to a third party who is close to you. Indirect upward communication can be easily overlooked if you are accustomed to "straight talk." Pay attention to indirect messages. Their very importance may be the reason they are not delivered directly. Create a safe environment for passing on feedback and new ideas.

Planning for the future

In a region pummeled by constant radical upheaval, it is difficult to foresee the future and even more difficult to plan for it. People in South America tend to be reactive rather than proactive; they focus on the present rather than the past or the future.

TIP

GIVE YOUR EMPLOYEES MORE ROOM
Imposing strict proceses risks stifling your workforce that has innate skills in innovation and adaptation.

Benefiting from innovation

South Americans do create long-term plans, which clearly lay out the strategic direction and the major milestones, but they determine individual steps as they are taking them. This provides the flexibility necessary in an uncertain environment. It also means that you must train and empower workers to respond and innovate as necessary. Of course, innovation can sometimes lead to risky short-cuts, so you need to prioritize procedures that are essential for safety and quality, balancing this with flexibility in procedures that are non-essential.

MEETING DEADLINES

FAST TRACK	OFF TRACK
Creating a sense of urgency about your needs	Expecting plans to follow a predetermined schedule
Sending frequent friendly reminders well in advance of deadlines	Not planning for last-minute emergencies
Being flexible about the route taken to your objectives	Letting your project slip down the priority list
Prioritizing essential procedures	Expecting a stress-free workplace

Creating a sense of urgency

With a focus on reaction rather than planning, it may seem that the entire day is spent putting out fires. Everything is urgent. A crisis is looming near the end of every day.And indeed, the work pace is often hectic. If you feel your requirements are being given a low priority, create a sense of urgency to bring them to the top of the list. Explain the absolute urgency of your need and how much you depend on the team to come through for you. Call daily, then check in for updates frequently. As the deadline truly looms, ask specific questions about what has been done and what is left to do. Do not underestimate your employees' ability to work overtime, to pull in extra resources, and to act intensely and with focus. South Americans work very hard to meet their commitments, and they can accomplish a project quickly when it becomes the priority.

TIP

TRACK RESULTS
Monitor progress through frequent verbal updates. Project managers will meet targets but will groan if you demand detailed reports.

Keeping priorities flexible

Focusing on the short-term may lead to detours as processes develop. For those accustomed to timetables and detailed guides, this may look like an undisciplined change of direction. But another perspective is that detours lead to new and better ways of accomplishing objectives and identifying new opportunities. The reactive style means people can see and seize new opportunities as they arise.

You can expect your employees actively to add to their portfolio, seeing new projects as additions rather than substitutions. You should not be threatened by detours, and allow them to take their course where they are not endangering your overall objectives or schedule. Yes, you may need to refocus and reprioritize frequently, but don't let a single-minded focus on initial objectives stifle the creative vision and adaptive skill of your South American partners.

Chapter 3

Succeeding at business

Once you have understood how business and society work in South America, you can move on to putting your plans into action. This requires understanding the practical aspects of logistics, finance, marketing, and negotiation. With these essentials and the right people on your team, you will be well positioned for business success on the continent.

Setting an entry strategy

South America is so diverse, one strategy will not work for the whole region. Consider using more than one channel, such as franchising, joint ventures, or licensing, to ensure the best fit for each location. Newcomers should start with one country or one city and expand only after achieving their objectives.

Distribution channels

*Sell in—
the transaction from manufacturer to retailer.

*Sell out—
the transaction from retailer to consumer.

To succeed in South America you will have to be flexible. You may have to use multiple channels that you would not think of using in your home country, such as franchising, door-to-door, agents, or telemarketing. Whatever channels you choose, it is quite probable that you will benefit by helping your partners with both sell in* and sell out*. Besides training them about your products and services, you will get best results if you also provide them with tools to manage their own businesses more effectively.

Joint ventures and franchising

You can acquire knowledge of your target location through a successful local partner who can offer insights and help you make quick adjustments in the changing environment. Spend time in target countries during the planning stages to get to know potential partners and the local culture. A joint venture partner will share your risk but will need time to get to know you.

Franchising is a form of joint venture that also allows for global standards with adaptations necessary for each region of the continent. The franchising market is quite sophisticated in Brazil, but is less so in other South American countries.

TIP

PARTNER WITH EXPERIENCE
A foreign-based partner with proven experience in the region may be your best bet when starting out because they will understand your concerns.

Licensing

Though manufacturing companies in South America may be eager for licensing contracts, many will be unprepared for the demands of working with a foreign partner. Expect to help your partner with appropriate investments in technology and business tools such as financial controls and key performance indicators. Many firms may be producing at capacity, but may be open to licensing if they get enough support from the foreign partner.

CASE STUDY

Using local knowledge

International fast-food chain Pizza Hut's attempts to open restaurants in São Paulo, Brazil, failed three times until they found a capable local partner to lead them to success. Jorge Aguirre changed Pizza Hut's image to make it a more desirable brand. He opened his first store on the same street as the city's most sophisticated restaurants. He hired beautiful hostesses and elegant waiters. He complemented the standard Pizza Hut toppings with new sophisticated toppings, many of them co-branded with respected local products such as Catupiry Cheese and Perdigão Turkey. His menu is a monthly magazine that diners can take home, and the restaurant is filled with with Pizza Hut stuffed bear mascots.

Getting started

Because South America is not an easy location for doing business, the best way to get started in the region is generally to start slowly. You should incrementally increase your investment and risk exposure only as you enjoy successes and learn how to do business in an uncertain environment.

Preparing for reality

South American business competition is tough, and you may find few antitrust or competition laws to protect you as a newcomer. In practice some South American countries may permit defensive moves like collusion, copyright infringement, and predatory pricing. Volatile business conditions are another factor to consider as you get started.

Staged entry strategies

1 IMPORT–EXPORT
Before you relocate, test your product by exporting to your target market. Both risk and investment will be low at this stage. Follow up initial success with a greater investment.

2 COOPERATION
Research is important, but South Americans recognize the value of "feeling" the right business move. A partner with local instincts and success will have developed this skill.

5 **LOCAL COMPANY**
Establishing a legal local entity
can be tedious, but the favor
you win with governments,
suppliers, and distributors can
be well worth the effort.

4 **DISTRIBUTORSHIP
AGREEMENTS**
Find a successful distributor in
the desired channels, and have
a local attorney draft a contract
that protects both parties.

3 **MAJORITY-OWNED
JOINT VENTURE**
This arrangement allows you to
gain local wisdom while keeping
strategic control. You will be
welcome if you provide funding
and respect local insights.

Taking a staged approach

A staged approach to South America may be the
best way to face the reality of the region. For example,
you might export your product first, then work with a
partner, then open your own manufacturing facilities. The
entry strategy you choose and the pace of expansion
depend on your risk tolerance and previous international
experience. But be warned, South America is not an easy
place for beginners in international business.

Dealing with infrastructure

Infrastructure and logistics still represent serious challenges when doing business in South America. Only some urban and more developed rural areas are well served with good energy supply, modern telecommunications, and complete logistics infrastructure.

PLAN AHEAD
Before doing business in South America, carefully analyze the precise logistics routes in regions where you will operate. Consider investing in your own private infrastructure to improve your efficiency.

Waterways and ports

Although many rivers cut across the region, inland waterways are underutilized in South America. In terms of maritime logistics, the port infrastructure in South America has reached its capacity limit due to increased international trade. Additionally, port operations are generally inefficient, with outdated technology causing frequent delays. The lines of trucks waiting to be loaded or unloaded can extend for miles and take days to clear. Port labor strikes are also not infrequent and can be very disruptive. Expect long and variable lead times when shipping to and from South American ports.

BE FLEXIBLE
With dramatic differences in regional infrastructure, maximize your logistics efficiencies in each area in which you operate. Don't expect one system to work everywhere.

Logistics infrastructure

• **Roads** Roads are by far the predominant mode of cargo transportation, but expect delays and traffic problems. The road network is mostly concentrated in Brazil and Argentina. On average, only 13 percent of the roads in the region are paved. The most efficient roads are privately-managed toll and secondary roads. Road cargo theft remains an issue in some areas.
• **Rail** Except for Paraguay, Bolivia, and parts of Brazil, the railroads do not play a significant role in South America for transportation. The Brazilian government has privatized some important segments of its railway system, resulting in a fast rate of improvement and consequent increase in demand and significance.

Energy and telecommunications

After large-scale privatization and increased market liberalization, the energy sector here is developing fast. The bulk of the energy generated is still hydroelectric, but future expansions will be based on large reserves of natural gas. Distribution remains a problem, but access to the energy grid has greatly improved in recent years, and most areas are now supplied with electricity. Similarly, the telecom sector has experienced a quantum leap in the availability and reliability of voice communication infrastructure, with good, extensive coverage for cellphone and landline networks. In terms of data communication, most urban areas are well served by broadband internet access, and virtually all countries have plans to improve access in rural and marginal urban areas.

TIP

RESEARCH YOUR OPTIONS

Compare costs for your entire operation when choosing a location—energy, transportation, and emergency alternatives, as well as labor and taxes.

Dealing with financial issues

Your access to local financing and the financial risks that you face will depend on your target location. The countries of South America form three groups based on the strength and relative stability of their economies. Chile and Brazil form the top tier, followed by Colombia, Peru, and Uruguay. The rest form a third tier, as reflected in their sovereign credit ratings*.

Financing your operation

*Sovereign credit ratings—*the credit worthiness of a sovereign entity or country that lets investors know the economic and political risk of investing in that country.*

For local financing options, the capital markets in South America are not as developed as those in the US or Europe. If you require local financial investment, the bigger countries such as Argentina, Brazil, Chile, Peru, and Colombia offer the best opportunities. However, money markets can be very volatile, due to the dependency of many countries on international investors for liquidity. Additionally, regulatory constraints can make relying on local finance costly.

Most South American companies rely on the banking sector for financing rather than on capital markets. However, banks in South America require significant collateral, due to stringent banking regulations which push financial intermediaries to demand guarantees sometimes far above the amount of the loan. Also, banks require personal and business references before issuing loans, and can be slow with approvals and even slower with disbursements.

However, once you have a good ongoing relationship with a bank, you can speed up the process and negotiate better terms. Plan ahead and initiate contacts well in advance of your forecasted needs. You should also be aware that banks in South America require that you repay any first loan before you can even request a second. In other words, you will not be able to roll over the principal.

TIP

NEGOTIATE DIRECTLY

To limit regulatory and tax change risk, negotiate investment agreements directly with the government. Work through their agency for the promotion of foreign direct investment.

Managing financial risk

You will face three major sources of financial risk when investing in South America: exchange rate risk, regulatory and tax changes, and the possibility of expropriation*. Exchange rate risk largely depends on how freely the local currency can be converted. In the past, some countries in the region have flirted with fixed exchange rates, and in this context you have to consider not the return, but rather in which currency you can take your profit. With free convertibility, you can hedge the currency risk on the international markets, a task easier to accomplish with the larger countries' currencies.

Regulatory changes and expropriation are unavoidable risks unless your project is large enough to qualify for political insurance from the United Nations (UN), the International Finance Corporation of the World Bank (IFC), or another multilateral agency. For some projects in South America, the IFC itself can be a source of financing This has the added advantage of providing you with some political safeguard: a government is less likely to expropriate an investment supported by the World Bank, as this might damage their own credit lines with the institution.

*Expropriation— action taken by a state to confiscate property, or to modify the rights of its owners.

TIP

BEWARE OF PUNCTUATION
Currency figures in South America use the comma and period the opposite of the way they are used in the US and UK. Two thousand dollars and twelve cents is written in figures as $2.000,12.

CASE STUDY

Finding the money

In 1997 two young men in Argentina founded Officenet with $50,000 provided by a local businessman. The company used a new and risky business model—selling office supplies through direct-marketing channels. The company became a huge success, and within six months the two founders had 22 employees and annual sales projections of $2 million. In 1998, the business attracted the attention of Endeavor, a network of venture capitalists and entrepreneurs specializing in emerging markets. Endeavor provided additional funds, training, and business consulting to help the organization develop. Officenet grew to employ 520 people and earn $57 million in annual revenue. In 2004, the company was bought by the multinational office supply chain Staples. The two founders now help other entrepreneurs get their ideas off the ground.

Importing and exporting

Despite talk of regional integration, trade agreements with South American countries are almost all negotiated bilaterally. Each country may have a string of agreements with individual nations. Foreign companies not supported by trade agreements with their country may still find great opportunities for trade in South America.

Moving goods

*Import substitution —a trade policy that places prohibitively high tariffs on imports in order to reduce external competition and push the growth of local industry.

Documentation and procedures for importing and exporting do not differ from those practiced elsewhere, although in some cases, the paperwork can be cumbersome. But the region has made huge strides in improving the efficiency of processing both imports and exports. Although the days of protectionist policies and import substitution* still ring in recent memory, today there are relatively few prohibitions for either import or export. Each country in South America maintains its own policies and you should research the local rules before filling your container and hauling it to the docks. Weak infrastructure and poor management of port logistics may create severe bottlenecks. Choose your ports carefully as there is significant variation both between and within countries.

MAIN IMPORTS AND EXPORTS

COUNTRY	EXPORT COMMODITIES	EXPORT PARTNERS	IMPORT COMMODITIES	IMPORT PARTNERS
Argentina	soybeans and derivatives, petroleum and gas, vehicles, corn, wheat	Brazil, China, US, Chile	machinery, vehicles, petroleum and natural gas, organic chemicals	Brazil, US, China, Germany
Brazil	transportation equipment, iron ore, soybeans, footwear, coffee	US, Argentina, China, Netherlands, Germany	machinery, transportation equipment, chemical products, oil, electronics	US, China, Argentina, Germany, Nigeria
Chile	copper, fruit, fish products, paper and pulp, chemicals, wine	China, US, Japan, Netherlands, South Korea, Italy, Brazil	petroleum products, chemicals, electrical equipment, machinery, vehicles, natural gas	US, China, Brazil, Argentina
Colombia	petroleum, coffee, coal, nickel, emeralds, apparel, bananas, cut flowers	US, Venezuela, Ecuador	industrial and transportation equipment, consumer goods, fuels, electricity	US, China, Mexico, Brazil, Venezuela
Peru	copper, gold, zinc, crude petroleum and petroleum products, coffee, potatoes, asparagus, textiles, fishmeal	US, China, Canada, Japan, Chile, Switzerland, Spain	petroleum products, plastics, machinery, vehicles, iron and steel, wheat, paper	US, China, Brazil, Ecuador, Argentina, Chile, Colombia
Venezuela	petroleum, bauxite and aluminum, steel, chemicals, agricultural produce, basic manufactured goods	US, Netherlands Antilles, China	raw materials, machinery and equipment, transportation equipment, construction materials	US, Colombia, Brazil, China, Mexico, Panama

Surviving bureaucracy

South American bureaucracy is best regarded as a form of overhead expense required for doing business in the region. While it is unavoidable, inconsistent, and slow, the bureaucracy is not insurmountable and patience and persistence should always see you through.

Dealing with red tape

A tangle of bureaucracy in South America has pushed companies to find ways around the rules, only to find more rules to fill in the exploited gaps. The result is tall stacks of forms, exploding numbers of regulating departments, and the need to spend days on end in government offices. You will save yourself a lot of frustration if you don't question the logic behind the arrangement, and simply explore the options in front of you.

MAKE CONNECTIONS
When your progress is slowed or stopped, personal connections can often lead you to someone who can help.

DO NOT BRIBE
Do not assume corruption is the norm. Bribery is illegal and offensive. A small gift of thanks, however, will be remembered.

Coping with bureaucracy

BE NICE
Treat every person with respect. Respect their authority to make demands and decisions. Act as though they are doing you a favor.

ARGUE PERSUASIVELY
Small exceptions can always be made if the reason is compelling and the person asking seems to deserve help.

KEEP RECORDS
Organized paper work speeds your delivery. And looking competent to officials may mean less scrutiny.

HIRE HELP
A lot of time may be spent waiting in lines. It pays to hire one of the professional firms that specialize in facilitating paperwork.

COMPLETE FORMS CORRECTLY
Small errors, sloppy presentation, and blank spaces are all reasons a clerk might reject your petition.

Tackling security

Due to extremes of wealth and poverty, crime rates are quite high in South America, especially in urban areas. Law enforcement is usually underfunded and understaffed, so companies and individuals must act to protect themselves. With reasonable precautions, most people encounter no more risk here than in other large cities around the world.

Recognizing trouble spots

Although there are frequent political strikes and marches, there is little violent civil unrest in South America. Terrorism is not a major concern, and most crime is committed for financial gain. Economic desperation coupled with generally inadequate police protection leave individuals and companies exposed to security risks. Wealthy neighborhoods located next to poor communities can be flash points. However, simple precautions can mitigate much of this risk.

TIP

STAY POPULAR
Good public relations with the local community will help to reduce the risk of crime. Good neighbors protect one another: if you look out for them, they will look out for you.

Ensuring personal safety

The best strategy is to avoid being noticed. Do not drive a luxury car or wear expensive jewelry. Avoid loud conversations in a foreign language because foreigners are assumed to be relatively wealthy. Carry only small amounts of cash and a copy of your passport.

If you are approached by strangers, be polite but move away quickly. Do not resist muggers, but hand over what they ask for. Make a police report afterward at your hotel or police station. Kidnapping foreigners is less common than kidnapping locals. It is too hard for criminals to communicate with those who would pay a ransom, and might involve foreign governments. A safe neighborhood should be the first priority in selecting hotels or homes.

Protecting business assets

In South America, companies must arrange for their own security assessment and protection, as the police may not be able to do the job. Professional services and consultancies are usually available to help.

Be sure you have systems and procedures in place that provide an adequate level of security for the specific needs of your company. To enter most office buildings, you will be asked to register at reception, show some form of identification, and maybe have your picture taken in exchange for a magnetic card that will unlock the turnstiles. Professional guards are a common feature in South American business districts, and their presence acts as a deterrent to potential criminals. Labor for security is relatively cheap, but you will need a system of incentives and controls for security personnel to prevent corruption. For further security, consider high-tech security systems, such as video-monitoring and tracking systems. Road cargo is quite vulnerable to theft, so hiring escorts and using tracking systems makes business sense.

✓ CHECKLIST PROTECTING YOUR ORGANIZATION

	YES	NO
• Have you assessed the security needs of your operations?	☐	☐
• Do you protect your people, facilities, and materials?	☐	☐
• Are your employees properly trained in safety and emergency procedures?	☐	☐
• Have you installed adequate monitoring and tracking systems for buildings and stock?	☐	☐
• Do you insure your cargo against theft in transit?	☐	☐

Starting a new business

South America is one of the most entrepreneurial regions in the world, but most of the entrepreneurial activity is driven by necessity and remains informal. However, innovation in business concepts and business practices is vital for success in the region, making the workforce well suited to the demands of entrepreneurial activity.

BE CREATIVE
Think creatively about ways to overcome bureaucratic constraints.

Preparing for the conditions

The bureaucracy in most South American countries is not favorable to small business. Most locals prefer the security of salaried jobs to the risks of starting their own business. Those who do start their own business may operate informally without proper documentation. There are penalties if they are caught, but some consider that a reasonable risk. For those operating legally, these informal businesses seem to have an unfair advantage. Brazil is considered the most difficult country for entrepreneurs, and Chile one of the best. Peru, Colombia, and Venezuela have the highest percentage of people owning their own business.

Innovating and investing

The combination of a difficult business environment and a population with adaptive skills makes South America a rich location for innovation. As a manager, you should not underestimate the problem-solving capacities of your colleagues. An entrepreneurial spirit within a company, called "intrapreneurship," can be one of the great advantages of the region. If you are looking to invest in local small businesses, remember that successful entrepreneurs require business skills as well as a bright idea. Local entrepreneurs may benefit from your business and management advice as well as funding.

Using resources

The rate of entrepreneurship in South America is high, but the failure rate is also very high. Your own personal dedication and resourcefulness are vital for success in any commercial ventures in the region. They say that if you can start a successful business in South America, you can expand anywhere after that! However, you can find help. Business schools can be useful partners if you want to launch a new business in the region. In almost every country in South America, business schools have established research and training programs as well as incubator projects to assist entrepreneurs. They will also have information about government programs and local investors.

Do not rely on finding local financial help. Most business ventures in South America are funded by contributions from family members, or seek loans from banks at home. Venture capitalists and angel investors are not common, although these resources are increasing as more investors become aware of the region's potential.

TIP

**KNOW
YOUR LIMITS**

The entrepreneurial personality and the personality suited to filing government documents are rarely found in the same person. Hire a good accountant or lawyer to help you.

ASK YOURSELF... CAN YOU LAUNCH YOUR BUSINESS IN SOUTH AMERICA?

- Do you have enough funding? The average investment needed in the region is about $15,000, compared to about $68,000 in other countries.
- Can you work with scarce resources?
- Do you have a good local lawyer or accountant to guide you through the bureaucracy and get through the formalities?
- Can you make quick decisions in an environment of high uncertainty?
- Are you flexible and creative enough to adapt and make changes in a dynamic external environment?
- Can you easily establish contacts and create a network of business relationships?
- Are you comfortable with some ambiguity about the legal way to do things?

Segmenting the market

Every market segmentation strategy in South America must consider the extreme differences of wealth and poverty, urban and rural areas, and values of the young and old. However, the most successful approaches combine segmentation criteria to understand and meet consumer needs.

TIP

CHOOSE THE RIGHT WEALTH MEASURE
High inflation, informal employment, and economic disturbances make "stock" measures, or what is owned, more reliable than "flow" measures, or what is earned.

Socioeconomic segments

Income distribution in South America is among the most unequal in the world, with a huge gap between rich and poor. The small wealthy class has enormous buying power and pays lavishly to get what it wants, giving excellent margins to retailers. However, this market is saturated and competitive. The new opportunities are coming from the middle class. This prime market was undersized and underserved, but the numbers are growing. Enjoying new prosperity, the middle class is driving consumption in the region. Ignored until recently, the lower-income sector is an attractive market because of its huge numbers. With no access to consumer credit, companies offering the poor monthly payment plans can attract loyal buyers.

CASE STUDY

Banking for the poor

With no credit history and little collateral, low-income consumers in South America usually have no access to financial services. Banco Azteca successfully entered Peru by extending a business model they developed for Mexico—targeting lower-income consumers, applying technology for efficiency, and building personal relationships for customer loyalty. Loan officers from Banco Azteca develop relationships with their clients, visiting their homes for a personal assessment to decide a reasonable loan amount. They return to clients' homes regularly to receive loan payments and may offer complementary products like life insurance and savings accounts. Home visits in congested neighborhoods are facilitated by sophisticated GPS systems, scheduling software, and company scooters.

Demographic segments

While income differences are critical, other market demographics should not be neglected. Gender differences are pronounced: women do the household shopping while men make major purchases. As more women enter the workforce, they are sharing in and making more decisions. Age is another important factor. In most countries of the region, almost half of the population is under 18 and less than 10 percent is over 65. Capturing the youth market can be profitable in the short and long term. Their lifestyles and values are not traditional. Retired parents may move in with their children and grandchildren. The "sandwich generation" spends to indulge both their children and their parents.

Geographic segments

In a region where getting products to customers may be challenging, distribution channels are a priority for market segmentation. Each country in South America usually has one huge metropolis. Easy access to millions make this segment the first choice for distribution. The next phase of growth is still focused on urban areas, but requires moving away from the metropolises. Second-tier cities may be hard to reach, but unmet demand and affordable real estate are good reasons to make the effort. Many rural consumers have some disposable income, but may not have basics like electricity, cars, and plumbing.

Lifestyle segments

Simple demographic segmentation is no longer adequate to explain the increasingly wealthy South American market. Combining different segmentation criteria can help companies tap into the hugely diverse market. Most lifestyle classifications of the region's consumers use a combination of socioeconomic class with values. For example, some lifestyle segments identified in Chile include socially active as opposed to home-focused, and economically aspirational against successful and fulfilled. Traditional and modern are also important lifestyle segments. Other ways of segmenting markets might be environmental priorities, peer or family focus, international views, health and fitness, or hobbies. Socioeconomic stratification of the metropolises used to be enough to reach a lucrative market. Today market segmentation must combine approaches for increasingly sophisticated consumers.

Income distribution

Socioeconomic classes in South America are assigned letters to differentiate them from each other. The official census department of each country decides how to determine the classification, but it is usually some combination of income, education level, and possessions owned such as a car, vacuum cleaner, and number of televisions. The table below explains some possible market segments.

POSSIBLE MARKET SEGMENTS				
	A	**B**	**C**	**D**
Lifestyle	Luxury	Comfortable	Have the basics	Struggling
Typical professions	Doctors, attorneys, engineers, executives	Managers, health care workers, small entrepreneurs	Laborers, office workers, employees at minimum wage	Day laborers with jobs such as cleaning, repairing
Typical level of ownership	Beach house, luxury car, designer clothes	Own home, car, appliances, some luxuries	Rent home, have basic necessities, use public transportation	Lack many basics like good shelter, warm clothing
Consumer behavior	Seek status, comfort, leisure	Seek good quality, buy some brands	Price sensitive, buy brands on occasions	Buy small quantities near home
Share of wealth	The A classes control about half the wealth of South America	Relatively small number of people with moderate wealth	Large number of people with enough to meet basic needs	D and E classes are 20–40% of the population, with just 10% of the wealth
Notes	Lucrative and demanding, saturated with luxury brands	Lifestyle similar to that of the middle class in US or Europe	This is the fastest growing segment	Living on a few dollars a day

Selecting a location

Due to great variation between countries and cities in South America, selecting a location in the region is as important as it is complex. Most organizations find it easier to establish themselves in one South American location successfully before moving to multiple locations.

Choosing a starting place

Identify a location with few regulations and a simple tax code for your industry. Competition in your industry may tell you that conditions are favorable. Among the competitors you may also find business partners and managers with invaluable local experience. Of course early success in a competitive cluster also means finding your unique niche without provoking established players who may react defensively. Check local antitrust and competition laws to see how much protection you can expect as a new entrant.

Managing location costs

Identify the main cost drivers for your company and industry. Supplies and costs of raw materials, facilities, space, and labor vary greatly throughout South America, as do taxes and tariffs. Because of uneven infrastructure, transportation can be a major cost differential between locations. Some of the less expensive locations in South America may have deficiencies that can be resolved through private investment—from building your own roads to providing housing for workers—with the added benefit that governments will welcome businesses aligned with their economic development programs.

TIP

START IN A LEADING MARKET
If your first location is known for having consumers who are trendsetters, or has a reputation for innovation or industry leadership, this can help speed your expansion.

Reaching your target market

Proximity to a significant concentration of customers can speed early sales success. You can find lots of eager consumers in cosmopolitan cities like São Paulo, Rio de Janeiro, Buenos Aires, and Santiago. Shopping malls in these cities are entertainment hubs for upper- and middle-class shoppers. But competition is intense here, and space is very expensive. New entrants may find better results in second-tier cities where the market is not yet saturated. Consider Lima, Bogotá, Quito, Montevideo, Belo Horizonte, Curitiba, and Salvador, although fast growth is already narrowing opportunities in these cities.

Targeting the middle class

If your target is middle-class consumers, you can find them in peripheral neighborhoods that ring the big cities, in smaller cities, and in rural areas. There is huge sales growth in this market, but also challenges in accessibility—both for distribution and for consumers. Middle-class retail is fragmented, with shops clustered on the streets around public transportation hubs such as subway stations. Security and supply chain logistics on the street are more challenging than in a mall.

✔ CHECKLIST SELECTING A LOCATION

	YES	NO
• Am I aware of local laws and regulations?	☐	☐
• Am I aware of local businesses that will form my competition?	☐	☐
• Will transportation to and from the region add greatly to my costs?	☐	☐
• Does the location have the infrastructure I need?	☐	☐
• Does the local population fit my target market?	☐	☐
• Do I have a back-up plan in case circumstances change?	☐	☐

Negotiating successfully

South Americans prefer to do business with people they like and trust. Formal negotiation may seem unnecessary among friends but it still clarifies specific activities. Negotiations do not have to be adversarial. Ideally you should approach negotiations as if you are all on the same side—you are each contributing to a common goal.

HOW TO... CONDUCT TALKS

Try to build positive regard between all parties.

↓

Send someone who can promise to execute.

↓

Send a team that matches the level of your counterparts.

↓

Make sure you know the laws of all countries involved.

↓

Identify who in the other party has the authority to make decisions.

Getting down to business

Negotiations in South America can be fast and emotional. People express themselves openly and may mistrust those who seem to be holding back. The focus of negotiations in South America tends to be on agreeing to general principles of a contract, not on the specific details of execution, so don't jump into the fine print until everyone is comfortable with the basic parameters.

Resist the temptation to be time efficient. Give yourself plenty of time to complete negotiations. This may mean a few days instead of a few hours. South Americans will focus on the task at hand and concentrate on working out a contract to everyone's satisfaction. If you are focused on finishing by a certain time, you may end up making more concessions than necessary because you are feeling time pressure while your counterpart is not.

Compromise is expected on both sides, so start your negotiations at a point that leaves plenty of room to move without passing your comfortable limits. Do not make concessions as these may be perceived as weakness; propose trade-offs that require both sides to move simultaneously. The most successful trade-offs will be those in which each party wins something important to them while giving up something less important. Know your own priorities and listen carefully so that you understand what matters to your counterpart.

Keeping it friendly

As you work through the various points in a negotiation, start with everything you agree about first. Don't skip these points just because they are easy. By agreeing repeatedly on many points, you establish a positive cooperation with your counterpart. Only after you have established a great rapport and long list of agreement should you broach the difficult points. In tense moments, you may want to take a break so that both parties can regroup. Focus on a win-win approach, working together on a common project for collaborative ends. You will be more productive and get better terms if you are perceived by your counterpart as being on the same team. Do not make power plays that make your counterpart seem weak or inferior. If offended or pushed too far, South Americans may abruptly cancel a negotiation no matter how much effort has been invested and how much potential reward could be gained. Negotiations are part of an ongoing relationship, not an isolated activity. If you don't negotiate reasonably, you won't be trusted to execute reasonably.

TIP

RESPECT THE OTHER PARTY
There is a lot of variation within South America and some negotiators may be more direct than others, but respect and courtesy are expected everywhere.

Documenting an agreement

The written contract in South America is still an important document, although it may be perceived more as a statement of expectations than as a specific promise to perform. No matter how solid, a contract is a living document that is managed throughout the relationship. If your counterpart insists on many disclaimers this may be a sign that they are not certain they can perform. Include dispute resolution in the contract itself, such as identifying a third-party arbitrator, or terms of a buyout. Independently verify all claims, as exaggeration is a common negotiating tactic and due diligence is the responsibility of each party.

Resolving disputes

Although South Americans prefer to do business with their friends, they recognize that even the best of relationships may suffer from misunderstandings. Avoid an outright brawl whenever possible, as serious disputes in South America have long-term consequences and may sever even long-standing relationships.

AGREE ON A VENUE

Jurisdiction is always a complex issue in international dispute resolution. Agree on a venue before there is a conflict and be sure it is part of a written contract.

Understanding the law

Each country in South America exercises its own sovereignty. When doing business in more than one country, you must comply with the laws in each country. It is wise to have local attorneys working with someone from your headquarters so that all interests and constraints are represented and understood. South American countries practice civil law, sometimes called code law. This is the same system used by most European and many Asian and African countries.

ACTIVELY MANAGE THE CONTRACT

A contract must be managed as it is executed. In this sense it is a living document, not a stone tablet of laws. Your South American partner will expect you to be flexible and practical over the life of a contract.

Applying the law

In civil law the primary authority for resolving disputes is a written code that lists guiding principles for conduct. As it is practiced in South American countries, civil law has some distinct characteristics from other regions. The law lays out a set of general principles that must be applied to specific cases by a judge. Much of a judge's responsibility is to decide which code is most relevant for a specific case. They may focus more on choosing which rule to apply than on the actual merits of a case. Since civil law mandates specific actions, cases can be won or lost on procedural issues. The winner of a dispute is often the side that best manipulates the procedural codes rather than the one with the most compelling factual arguments.